A Happy Place

Tripti Jagasia Bakhtiani

BookLeaf Publishing
India | USA | UK

Presentation by *BookLeaf Publishing*

Web: www.bookleafpub.com

E-mail: info@bookleafpub.com

ISBN: 9789363300842

First edition 2024

To my parents, Kishore V. Jagasia

& Neelu K.Jagasia,

You are my universe and mean God to me.

It is your love, care & encouragement that

has made me who I am today; I am forever

grateful for the life you have given me to

explore and embrace.

I love you both more than life itself.

To my brother, Gautam K. Jagasia, Thank you

for being the best big brother, best friend,

cheerleader, teacher & protector. You are

always there for me,

You are a blessing. Bhaiya, I love you.

To my Sister-in-law, Deepika G. Jagasia,

I cannot thank you enough for recognising my

skills, visions

and helping me aim for them.

Thank you for being the most thoughtful,

courageous, fun and the coolest – mother,

daughter, elder sister and friend.

To my second set of parents (in-laws), Gobind A. Bakhtiani & Kavita G. Bakhtiani, Thank You for accepting me for who I am and pushing me to believe in myself. I love you both dearly.

To my husband and best life companion, Pawan G. Bakhtiani, you are everything I need! Thank you for your unconditional support, honesty, love and motivation. You make me fall in love with you every day, you make me like me every day.

Preface

A *Happy Place* is a collection of heartfelt poems and my humble attempt to capture the essence of beautiful elements of our lives that shape us and aid us in making this world a better place to live in.

Each poem in this book is a reflection of my journey, woven with the threads of personal experiences and the wisdom they brought. I have discovered that life's simplest moments often hold the most profound truths, like the bonds that inspire us, the lessons that guide us and the dreams that carry us forward.

As you turn through these pages, I hope they inspire you to reflect on your own experiences, cherish your connections, spark a joy and find your own happy place.

Thank you for letting my words be a part of your world.

With gratitude and love,

Tripti Jagasia Bakhtiani

The First Happy Place

When you open your eyes and can't understand things,

Two beautiful faces swing around with invisible wings.

You are embraced with warmth when crying for reasons you don't know,

Your smile and giggles light up their world,

Every day is a blessing for each time you grow.

Scared and confused,

You explore in glances towards distinct surroundings,

Solely you are reassured by recognisable voices that are purely comforting.

Their absence makes you upset,

And out comes a colourful dancing puppet!

Your first crawl towards them melts their hearts,

All that is known, that this is just the start.

Like jumping monkeys, they please you to utter your first word,

Irrespective of 'Mah-mah or Pah-Pah', you are simply adored.

Wandering in awe, sitting on a seesaw,

What is this weird sensation that you want to redraw?

A feeling so new and exciting,

You swing to heights, always in their sight,

Through a touch, or just their presence, you feel safe,

A notion of security that is only making you brave.

Like the inspiring chronicles you hear at bedtime
for a sweet sleep,

Pah-Pah protecting you and Mah-Mah –

From animals & monsters that can never sneak,

Memories like these are sure to keep.

Time goes by so swiftly,

Felt like you were born just a day before,

Oh! So small and pretty!

You are a prayer, a grace the universe answered,

Parents are your first happy place,

Forever to be treasured.

Colour Blind

Imagine a world that doesn't know what colours are...

Every day would be dynamically beautiful,

Everyone would be a star!

Imagine a world that doesn't understand colours;

We would take them as they are,

Bright, pastel, neon, dark, sparkled,

Textured or scarred.

We wouldn't know if they were warm or cold,

Nor yellow, mustard, orange, tan or gold.

There wouldn't have been discrimination by categories, types or mediums;

They would simply blend into our lives like art, music & poems.

Imagine a world that doesn't know what colour you are;

Experiences would lead to what we feel for each other.

Every day, each person would be dynamically beautiful,

Everyone would be a star!

Imagine a world that doesn't understand what colour you are...

We would take each other as we are;

White, fair, dark, wheatish,

Pink, blue, yellow, pale or scarred.

Imagine a world that doesn't know what colour we are;

No discriminations, judgements, superiority, inferiority, classism, types or categories;

Only valuing each other through our stories,

A life like sacred ivories.

What if we create a world that disapproves of identifying humans through their colour?

Every day, You and I would be zesty & beautiful,

You and I would be a rockstar!

All of us would take each other as we are,

We are all black, pink, yellow, blue, green,

silver and even bizarre!

Our children would only see colours as they are,

Skin would be skin, flesh would be flesh;

Only love, respect, humanity and progress.

Let's create a world that is colourblind...

To create a Happy Place with real colours,

Colours that give peace to the heart & mind.

Can you imagine a world that doesn't know what colours are?

Let's be colourblind.

Playground Delight

Framed with rustic mesh,

Stands a magnificent royal entrance.

Yellow sitting benches and colourful fences,

Bright green pastures bordered by pathway strips,

This is the gateway to joy, love and friendships.

A huge water fountain with music & light in focus,

Large animal statues in poses.

Voices of people and children buzzing,

Oh, how magically welcoming!

All known faces are here,

Your friend's name you overhear;

Hopping and jumping, hugged and greeted with excitement,

It's time to show your sporty talent!

Tiny legs running on green fluffy grass,

Chasing each other, next is your chance,

Hide & seek, hopscotch and tag,

All games must be played with points in track.

Parents & nannies eagerly waiting with your snack bag,

Exhausted, you take a short break;

Sitting in a big circle, sharing nibbles, stories and brags,

Energy is regained and the mind is awake,

Together you all rush to the playground; it is a craze!

Kids waiting in line to try each of their favourite play;

Swing, see-saw, merry-go-round and slides,

Rock climbing, tube slides and spring rides!

Giggling and laughing,

Laying on the grass and rolling,

You see your grandmother from far, staring.

The bright blue sky is now turning dark,

The sun has set,

You realise what time it is and take slow steps.

Praying and wishing this day never ends,

Alas! You are called upon, and your hand has been held.

The bags are packed,

You are being dragged,

Laying on the ground, trying to stop & yell,

Ah, what a cute rebel!

You are reminded to visit tomorrow again,
And are promised of yummy candies & balloons,
You wipe your tears and hum happy tunes.
Now that's a moment of zen!

Hopping your way home with candy in one hand,
And balloons in the other;
What a beautiful moment, you wonder.
These playground delights must never be missed,
Precious and pure happiness forever, you wished.

A simply magnificent gate is now closing in,
Playground delights must be pledged,
As a never-ending mission.

To be soon visited again, no matter what age,
For all feelings dwelling that are shy and strange.
You wipe your tears again and hum happy tunes,
You have crossed years and even dunes;

Awaiting to enter through a magnificent royal gate,

Thinking and sulking, is it too late?

And pastures will forever be green,

Colourful fences, yellow benches are still to be seen;

You are a child for life,

For love and a happy place, you thrive,

To enjoy and witness again,

This playground delight.

Different Doors, Different Homes

Bags are packed, done rightly so and strapped;

Reservations in hand,

You are ready to experience the land!

Through a car, bike, train, plane or ship,

You want to be on time; nothing can be skipped.

With family, friends, strangers, tour groups or solo,

The excitement and hope in your heart,

Are to keep your nerves mellow.

Seats are reserved for being guided by tracks,

Befriending strangers and sharing snacks.

For if a flight you picked,

Tickets are scanned and held,

Be careful,

Screen your belongings & laptops separately,

Or the security will yell!

Boarding freely after the check,

Greeted by attendants,

You can't wait to relax your neck!

Off you take, with silence around you,

No strangers to befriend here,

Free snacks are just for a few!

Flying through the fluffy clouds,

Are screaming babies and parents like clowns.

A home away from home, you are wanting;

As time passes by, it's morning!

Dragging your luggage, you begin an adventure,

Securing a safe ride over to your favourite leisure.

What is your pick?

A cosy homestay, hotel or a luxury kick?

Whether at a local's abode,

Or a majestic resort suite,

Fill your heart & belly with delicacies and
mouth-watering treats!

Walking and exploring the roads unknown,

Enjoying the animal safaris, evening bonfires and
collecting river stones,

The grace of their hospitality will never make you
feel alone.

A dream it was that you desired,

Listening to stories unheard and wired.

Through the lush mountains, with a drop of snow,

You breathe in the soothing greens, open blue
skies,

The air is so chilly, a fog you can blow.

A dream it was you desired,

To chase waves till you get tired!

Watching the sun rise and set,

On your beach bed, you lay your head.

Rhythmic sounds of the waves;

By a skyline with dreamy shades,

This is your Happy Place.

The ocean, a natural therapy for the mind, body and soul,

Your heart is content again, feels whole.

When cultures differ, art & music bind,

And sometimes even meet personalities with like minds.

Every path you take, discards all your doubts;

Meeting warm canines with angelic spirits,

Making you pout.

Every step you take to enter a world you never knew,

After ravishing moments, memorabilia you brewed.

From postcards, stamps, fridge magnets or brands,

Your pockets & shoes will always find ample sand.

With every ticket booked,

And every transport boarded,

You give away a lot of your old self,

Earn memories & experiences like gold & wealth.

Take a chance and create your happy zone,

Risk a breath and welcome,

Different doors, different homes.

What You Say

To think deeply before you share,

In happiness, love, rage or despair.

Worn by feelings and tone that are bare,

Can ruin life or make someone's day;

Your words matter and what you say.

Trust the power of words and its valour,

It can make one believe, misinterpret or keep them in the blur.

Use the magic of words and its bravery;

Take away the chaos and fill the world with colour, making it pretty.

Foresee the actions your words can draw,

Unite or break, reveal the truth and fake,

Express the reality, not convey the wrong,

It is our choice of words that can make one succeed or fail,

Winning over with motivation & smile,

Even when pale.

So, think deeply before you share,

In joy, passion, anger or pain;

What you say will always be rare,

There are cold hearts you must repair.

Let's create strong minds free from manipulations,

That are not lured through money, power,

Whips and guns to take over the nation.

What you say can spread love or hurt,

Or build a world that is happy,

Wise, cared for and heard.

The City I Live In, The City I Love

Blessed by Goddess Maha Amba,

This attractive 'Good little bay',

A land by and for the Kolis;

Their humility, culture & food will make one sway.

Ruled over and captured by dynasties,

Stolen from royalty & corrupted by Sultanate, Portuguese & British;

Exhausted, this tiny urban palace rises and flourishes.

Combined with seven islands, a place that never sleeps,

Exuberant with the Arabian Sea as its heart and nerves as creeks,

With big dreams and stressed goals,

The people that live here are the soul.

Mesmeric, crowded beaches with delicious street food carts and witty hawkers,

Large wholesale markets to multinational corporates with massive headquarters.

Selling big Bollywood fantasies,

The film hubs with no boundaries;

The city I grew up in, this city I love,

Inspires in different ways when life is tough.

Walls of historic forts and carvings of ancient caves,

Eye-catching are even the railway stations, municipal houses & fancy names.

Adored by the government & small towns, the world decides to settle here,

In humongous numbers, wanderers rush in for travel & carriers;

The city was barely groomed to shelter so many people,

Or geographically prepared, it's fairly clear.

Yet endures criticisms & furies of strangers that enter its abode,

These strangers looking for food, roof, labour, wealth, love and fame,

Welcomed with open arms & small houses that are weakly built & framed.

Trends are ideated, rolled out, broken and reformed,

This legend is booming to keep you warm & warned.

Monuments turned into luxury hotels,

Race cars on wrecked roads driven by regrets.

Parties on skyscrapers, pictures at fancy bars,

A line of shady beer houses with local mafias & struggling stars.

You will find a variety of distractions here,

Nothing has been spared,

From malls, theatres, national parks to lakes,

Corporate hubs & galleries, art & food fests and sea-facing promenades;

An easy target for grenades and crime that is beyond repair.

Mainly a Mumbaikar with a ghost of a Bombayite,

If you are confused, just ask and we will be your guide.

Once you stay here, your lungs & breath will get used to it,

You will cheer for the city performing in the IPL with pride,

Leaving your ego in splits.

With accent and lingos that are captivating,

The common man here is the real King.

Everyone here is in a haste and hurry,

No one here cares about who your father is or how you earn your money.

From talent displays on evenings at Carter Road to morning bhajans in local trains,

There are a million things to explore and indulge in;

Connects and contacts here are made conveniently for a gain.

Beggars here are rich,

With accounts in Swiss,

Daily labourers sleeping on sidewalks & dividers
all worked up and wasted,

Trying our best to be a clean city with paintings
on public walls spat on & decoded,

Green pastures in societies with vertical gardens
in narrow balconies;

A heaven in our small flats we have doted.

Roads poorly done, gutters flowing and potholes
countless,

Breathtaking views and beautiful sunsets at
Queen's Necklace.

No matter which part of the town you stay, there
is a sense of security,

Broad & caring minds make the nightlife safe even
for the drunk and tipsy.

This 'mayajaal nagri', no, an alpha world city,

Chill with us and hear stories that are
extraordinary.

A financial, commercial & entertainment capital,

Gets smaller and smaller by the fraction.

Famous as metropolitan, cosmopolitan with the highest number of billionaires,

Tower buildings and huge commercial prospects neatly glare.

A many reasons for migrant opportunists to enter the city & dwell;

In consequence, it became the most populous city, globally declared.

You can complain all you want about the traffic & the weather,

Costly lifestyle expenses to bear and investments to measure;

The rudeness and crudeness, illegality and bruteness,

You decided to be a part of the city & its chaos,

Why not live in happiness?

Between all the hustle and bustle,

Calmness and silence will be found in the noisiest of mental bubbles,

Moody passengers in their sound gears;

Shutting the world around them if solo,

Or intensely conversing in groups with their travel peers.

From jam-packed locals & metros, sluggish buses & monorail,

Experience an array of mixed cultures like a long movie unveiling in detail,

After a long, hard day, unwind with friends over a cocktail.

By the Taj and Gateway of India,

Or a beach walk at Juhu or Versova;

Take a break from the hectic and watch the sun set,

Enjoy the complementary jingles & background scores of beverage sales & head massage requests.

Yes, we love *pav* with our bhajiyas, wada and food,

Our sweet and spicy pani puri & fusion street chaat will set you in the right mood.

This is Mumbai, with generous hearts and random smiles,

If you are feeling lonely, don't succumb to your bad time;

Mumbai is very optimistic; 'It's okay re', is our favourite line.

Equality is a vibe,

Be your true self here; no need to hide.

There is something about the Mumbai air,

Sweat all day long, and you will still end up with good hair.

Here we boast about how long we were stuck in traffic or how many rides we had to miss,

Everyone understands how to mind their own business.

A sick-happy feeling,

You will not feel like leaving.

This happy place I was born in,

Huge residencies replacing lush gardens and greens,

This happy place is a total win.

No matter what, our spirit never dies,

This happy place, Mumbai, I call,

Is beyond and more than just money walls,

This city I live in is the city I love and adore.

Confidence

Unaware, and we are all born with it,

It begins with what seems familiar to us,

But disappears in darkness, in an uncertain hush.

As kids, we had only questions and no doubts,

Our family was our solution, a comfort zone with ups and downs.

The first day of school was scary with strangers all around,

We would whine and cry, run and hide until a friend was found.

With time, our fears of odd places and people healed,

Then we found ourselves between homework, exams, competition and nervous streaks;

Sports, art, hobbies and friends kept us at ease,

Extra curricula, debates & dancing on the stage, made us scream!

As we grew, we learnt to be ourselves,

Enjoying what we like and pursuing it was up our sleeves.

What interests you, will make you grow,

Fall in love with it and go with the flow.

In our dreams, we rock,

We can drive, dive, succeed and shock!

Only we can help ourselves and throw away the mental block.

When we wake up, we have to face the reality,

On bright days, we are tired and sleepy.

There are days we are very low,

What will happen in the future?

Will I make it, and how will it go?

Our minds filled with doubts and questions,

Overthinking and negative thoughts are our instant weapons.

When hit, failures make us feel weak, a zero,

We cut off from our parents, who were once our superheroes.

There are days we decide to complete what we started,

The next minute, we just don't feel like it,

Locked back in the closet.

Getting out of the bed feels scary,

Just a few more hours of sleep to feel healthy.

Reminded that these moments won't come again,

Let the calm blinking light in you help guide you,

So, rest well and understand that sometimes we need a break to regain.

The world in your head is at a standstill,

You are lost and the time doesn't stop,

Don't stop dreaming, for that is the key to your will.

Self-esteem isn't learned from the womb,

It takes scratches, beatings from life to bloom.

Just one step out of the bed,

And you will be out of your cold, heavy head.

The drops of warm water during a shower,

Will be the fresh start you were wanting to regain your power.

Just one step out of your zone,

Wear the colour that elevates your throne.

Eat your favourite food to feel happy & strong,

A walk in fresh air or bath in the pouring rain,

Listen & dance to your treasured playlist with peppy songs;

Trust yourself, take a deep breath and create a plan that stays for long.

Make yourself a promise,

To never look down on yourself ever again,

Believe in you, for you are a precious gem.

Treat the soul with love,

Hold yourself with courage,

Break free from your mind that keeps you captive.

Pamper your heart and make it so sturdy,

No person, situation or challenge will make your world shake or jerky;

You are your own strength; you are your own saviour,

Grip yourself high in your own regard and become braver.

Learn from the mistakes and experiences,

For there is no teacher greater than life;

You will feel confident about anything and everything,

And wear an armour suit in gold that makes you shine.

Your confidence is your happy place,

Don't complain and fight.

Like a beam of light, you will always matter,

Highlight your affirmations in your heart with a permanent marker;

Your confidence will never leave your side,

Confidence is what will keep you safe and secure forever, and it is your pride.

The Mentor

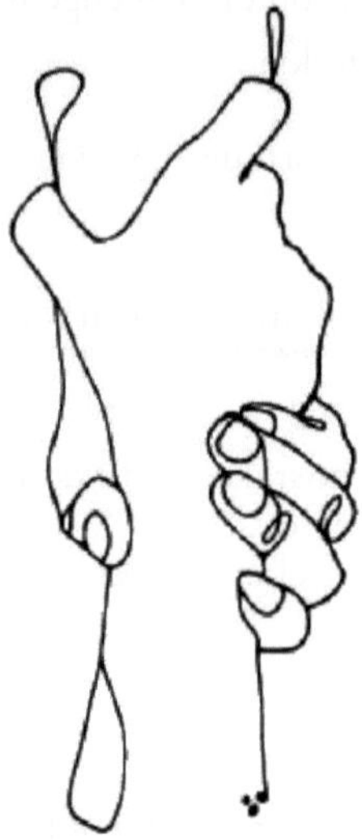

A need to grow,

Dreams you have sowed,

A call to test the waters of knowledge and life,

But no paths you know.

Lost in confusion,

With zero solutions,

Do you have a goal?

A need to grow,

For the dreams you have sowed,

Clasp the hand that can shepherd the way,

All you need is to be a protégé.

A guide to answer your why's,

To lead you out of the grey.

Their teachings, mistakes and expertise they share,

Abundance of insight and wisdom you obtain;

The will to choose the best, you earn;

Wise and strong decisions to make, you learn.

Mentors enter our lives in a variety of forms,

Like parents who answer all our questions,

The father, teaching us about life and lessons.

Being our pillar, making us brave and aware,

The mother who treats us with love and care;

Grooming us with upright etiquette, world civilities,

Recognising our skills,

Empowering us with precious abilities.

Such as the personal tutors who devote their time,

Helping us ace the syllabus, language refined.

Like the school, where we find long-lasting relationships,

Topics and subjects that make severe impressions.

The college that induces true competition,

A new world of interaction and projections,

Visiting faculties guiding us towards correct occupations;

Shifting of wavelengths and friendships, a surreal reminiscence.

Like the first job that taught us teamwork and what truly is ambition;

A mentor we find in our co-workers, bosses, a real transition.

Learning the value of time, multi-managing and upgrading our closets;

Having new aspirations by travelling for business conferences,

From overcoming the fear of asking questions to constructive decisions.

For the time, you are an ideal protégé,

Growing to be free even as expectations are at rage.

Grasping every encounter that is significant,

Presenting new ideas to writing our own stories;

Being responsible and taking it easy on worries.

Finding salvage through the art of solo travel,

Learning to love ourselves first and healing insecurities that are tangled.

Enhancing skills and keeping up with professional trends,

Finding our happy place every day by making amends.

Our teachings stay with us for an eternity,

If you don't get to be a protégé,

Life would be lost, with no harmony.

A boss is a mentor with a guiding light,

Firm, wise and will always be by your side.

With words that inspire to act and upskill,

A great boss turns work into bliss, an experience full of thrill;

They will help you spread out your wings to fly,

Their belief in you will make you touch the sky!

With patience, they plant values you need;

To grow and become what you are meant to be;

A mentor will make you strong, from weak.

A need to grow,

For the dreams you have sowed,

Clasp the hand that can shepherd the way,

Where wisdom flows like sun rays,

A mentor is a precious gift, an eternal enlightening bouquet.

Pluviophile

Best start to the day,

Surroundings graced to bright green from dull and grey,

Flowers blooming, birds chirping and animals in full sway;

Rhythmic sounds of the pour,

Calming my soul.

The blissful scent of the soil,

Urges me to place the tea to boil.

Oh, don't you just love the rain?

Scanty, heavy, windy, stormy and of all kinds?

I am a pluviophile and adore every bit of it,

I find it divine.

Monsoon is my favourite season,

And for so many and every reason.

Rushing into an open space,

Like the park, veranda or terrace,

Feeling content in getting drenched;

The delightful feeling as if the clouds are in my embrace,

When it rains, that is my Happy Place.

As a kid, rains would surprise me,

Shopping for raincoats and shoes, I would be on a spree!

With every lightning and thunder,

Why is everyone so afraid, I would wonder;

Praying to rain gods to pour heavily, in double,

Without giving the world any trouble,

So that schools and offices declare a holiday,

And I can spend the day with my family and enjoy it like a Sunday!

I would eagerly wait to jump in the muddy puddles,

Playing football with friends in the empty, slippery garden,

Falling and laughing, what a muddle!

Not worrying about getting my clothes dirty,

If it starts to drizzle,

To get soaked, I was ready!

The nostalgic smell of raincoats still gets me excited,

To binge on freshly prepared garam bhajiyas and vada pav with tea, is much needed.

Even today, over a gloomy day,

While some crib of traffic, bad weather and want it to go away,

The rains lift up my mood,

Enticing me to watch the nature boom,

Appreciate it with my heart full, all glued.

Whether at home or at work,

When travelling or driving with windows blur,

It makes me happy and secure,

Doing the things I love, writing my mind, dancing,

I am on a magical mental detour.

The pitter-patter music in the background is inspiring,

Encouraging me to dream, love, live and spin.

The exact weather,

For lounge attires to be worn for relaxation and pleasure,

The perfect climate for a romantic date,

To execute a plan to bunk work, class or college, what a great escape!

Indulge in a trip to the waterfall with a scenic view,

Old Monk with friends, old and new,

Profound conversations and ghost stories brew.

Between chilly winds and misty roads,

In a cosy cottage, singing songs and frosty toes;

The rains always make up for great memories and rainbows.

Though sometimes this season does cause distress,

To the lives of those who are unfortunate, causing accidents and tense,

I wish we took better care of this glorious planet,

A government body more prepared and crafted;

At every drop, a grumpy person would smile,

Every one of us would be a pleased Pluviophile.

Beach-laxation

Sunrise and sunsets,

Astonishing silhouettes.

Waves rising, wanting to reach the moon,

Blue sky, fluffy clouds hovering in tune.

Sparkling ocean,

Rough, yet calm motions.

Hues of sea blue and sea green,

How soulful this feels.

With tides high and low,

Our hearts beam and glow.

Three elements dancing together,
Water, human and sealife composed in nature.
A cocktail ambience,
Nothing more gorgeous,
Purple and pink blending with orange,
Mind healing, dump the baggage.
Sounds of children playing,
Nomads singing,
Hippies living,
Teenagers – busy clicking.
Colourful beach chairs,
Old bodies, bare.
Warm rays,
Trance caves,
Only silent are the waves.
Seashells and starfishes hanging out by the bay,
Hatchlings chasing the ocean in May.
Head and foot massages,
A dip in the deep,

Enjoy the free washes.

Reservations are a race,

Beach, a Happy Place.

Sting rays and jellyfishes,

Catching on for kisses,

Sun tans and sarongs,

Relishing beer and prawns,

Bracelets and anklets being sold,

Ravers all stoned.

Hot Hot Sun,

So much fun,

Awaiting sundowners,

At overrated cafes with expensive covers and big bouncers.

Beautiful beach view from a shack,

Don't want to go back.

Infinity adult-only pools,

Watermelon mojito is fuel.

Water villas with slides,

Speed boats and banana rides.

360-degree relaxation,

Vitamin sea, what a sensation!

Breakfast with views scenic,

These good days will never make you sick,

Go to the beach, it is a delightful tonic.

Leh Chalo

Body covered in warmers,

Pockets filled with camphor.

Dry fruits stocked,

Hand gloves, monkey caps and woollen socks.

Travel light,

Book a window seat for the flight;

Magnificent Ladakh range views await, what a sight!

No selfies and pictures you can take after landing,

The army can confiscate your phone and leave you hanging.

Excitement cannot wait,

Alas, a day or two needed to acclimate.

Monasteries and cultures to explore,

Fresh air in abundance is assured.

Clear skies,

Riders on bikes,

Caring locals with welcoming smiles,

Cold weather and warm delights.

Pleasant with quiet grace,

Like the heaven has opened its gates,

Oh Leh, you are a happy place!

Om Mani Padme Hum flags,

Fresh apricots, rugs, mats & hemp bags.

Chilly Pangong, crystal clear lake,

Snow mountains with mystical traits.

Valleys of Nubra,

Nights with the galaxy widely spread with countless novas,

Witness at night half of the globe,

Trust me, you won't need a telescope.

The abode of God so lucid,

Air so pure, unlike the city, polluted.

Look up in awe, and don't shake your head,

Tears of happiness will roll down as you lay in bed.

Momos, thukpa, kebabs,

Butter tea, khambir and pop art.

Try the food,

Every day is a good mood,

Culture and dance on display,

No bars, only cafes.

Starry nights,

Spiky heights,

Roads with angel guides;

Jhabro dance and camel rides,

Markets crowded with tourists that glide.

Visit once,

It heals your heart & lungs,

Discover in all its way,

Forever in Ladakh you would want to stay.

Phir Leh chalo...

Jahaan saans le paun... beh-jhijhak,

Phir le chalo, jahaan zameen bhi utni hi saaf ho jitna aasmaan...

Phir le chalo... wahin jahaan log bhi utne hi meethe ho jitna wahan ka paani,

Chalo, Leh chalein,

Wahin jahaan likh paaun ek aur kahaani.

Life is the King

Majestic and grand,

Reigns with a golden hand,

Born wearing a crown of dreams,

At times generous and occasionally mean;

Weaving experiences of joy and sorrow,

Destiny and luck creating music on piano.

Leader by birth,

Believe in its worth,

Faith aligned, trust the words.

A teacher for eternity,

Commanding at every opportunity,
Winning day-to-day battles,
Decorating the palace with medals.
Swimming through streams of doubts,
Fighting mindless storms in the scorching sun,
Wiping out negativity with optimistic guns.

Confidence, the only attitude,
When things go well, share your gratitude;
In laughter and tears,
With high hopes, conquering fears,
Breathing in supremacy,
Living lavishly.
Strong willpower and self-pride,
Teaching lessons in every step, forever a guide.

Protecting the mental peace,
Letting go of enemies,
Caring for memories;

Sometimes a destroyer, many times a saviour,

Standing for justice, rescuing from danger,

Spreading love, a natural creator.

Bow to its rule and cherish its grace,

For your life is the king of a happy place.

Art

At the break of dawn or as the world sleeps,

In places hidden, where no one can peep;

Sitting in silence, between memories & clutters,

Inspiration strikes, no words uttered.

With depth and focus beyond the surface,

Crafting something that is my own,

While this place and the people still feel unknown.

An echo of my salient heart,

Shaded with feelings of wondrous stark.

A language that needs no words to read;

Speaking through colours of red, blue, green.

Mirror of self, dreams unspoken,

A bridge towards calmness, golden.

Every stroke unfolding a story,

Hues drifting and dreamy.

Like caged birds set free,

Vision of a different planet, I see.

Come and find out what lies within,

Dive deep in yellow, white and mint.

Feel the textures,

A colourful treasure;

Follow the motifs,

Art is therapeutic; it keeps you at ease.

Pulse of the living world,

Actioned, restored and well preserved;

Illustrating history,

A famous trend or personality.

More than a pretty face,

Art is an ode to your happy place.

From ordinary and dull,

To dynamic and mystical;

Breathing life into your space,

Passersby halt and gaze.

In mind the magic lies,

Skills to execute and analyse;

More than brush, paint, paper and clay,

Truth and beauty unravel their play.

Without art, the world is cold,

A script incomplete, an anecdote untold.

Let's create a masterpiece,

An Art piece that the world needs.

Musicophile

As a wake-up alarm and when the phone rings,

During morning walks, gymming or running,

As a caller tune, even the caller sings.

In the shower, or while cooking in the kitchen,

On the way to work or travelling,

When creating art and brainstorming.

For road trips and long flights,

During house party gatherings or clubbing,

Music brings me unfathomable delight.

When I listen to it, I am a champion
Music is my beloved companion.
It is the pleasure for the pain,
Even in heavy rain or fast trains.

For every mood,
Happy or sad,
For children crying,
Winners high riding.
Beats to dance and groove;
Vocalists and their metronomes.
For tasks and performances,
As fillers or moves;
Catering to all seasons,
There is a song for every reason.
For movies and social media,
Advertising and euphoria.
Alone at home and stuck in a zone,
On the move, or in Rome;

For breakups and proposes,

Of lovers and roses,

For places and experiences,

Silent desires and romantic sequences.

As a musicophile, I can feel my wings.

Classical, jazz, blues and rock & roll,

Funk, folk and heavy metal,

Reggae, hip-hop and instrumental,

Techno, electronic and trance,

Pop, house, deep chill and dance

Electronic, country and indie,

Oh, the genres are so many!

Embrace the global harmony,

Listen to world music; you will go crazy!

In every corner of this globe, far and wide,

Rhythm awaits its devoted guide.

Music makes the world a happy place,

Making it reachable even through space.

Music is for all ages,

Young, old, saints and sages;

A fusion of cultures, wild and free,

Each note a thread, music weaves.

Bustling streets of Soho, Hong Kong,

The music there marks it as vibrant and warm;

African drums energetically calling,

Sitar strings sprawling.

Every lullaby has a story to tell,

Playing since ancient times,

Music will live till glaciers melt.

A lover of music, pure and true,

In every tune & symphony,

I have always found something new.

Music makes me fall in love with myself,

If blessed with this skill, you will excel.

Lose yourself in its flow,

Let your spirit glow;

It is the solace,

With so much grace;

It is present in hymns and prayers,

Caressing your heart, giving you tears.

Music is the ocean of wealth,

In grief, loss and even death.

Music will live forever,

Promising to never cease,

It is for the soul,

Soaking in all the peace.

I am thankful to all the musicians, writers, composers and artists,

I am a musicophile and forever blessed.

I cannot imagine a world without music,

It makes the world a happy place,

Music is a mystical life-saving tonic.

Freedom

Everyone's perspective on freedom varies,

Chiefly inspired by need and responsibilities,

Influenced by dreams, culture, age & societies.

For it is freedom you speak about,

Not to be confused with independence,

They both have different dimensions.

If you want to get out of your shell,
When home feels like a cage,
And living feels like hell;
If a change is what you desire,
For gains personal or future brighter;
You are seeking independence.

Who are you? And who am I?
Is this my purpose?
Who am I below this surface?
When you slowly get away,
When 'normal' feels astray;
When you see things as they really are,
Beneath the disguise, as a whole;
From surface to depth;
You search, ask, read and beg,
Questions lead you towards answers that feel like a threat.

Freedom is a Happy Place,

Full of incomplete resolutions scattered in a maze.

With solutions that are tough,

With Isolation like choking cigarette puffs.

Irrespective of your actions and decisions,

You feel no need to over-explain,

Closures and confessions are out of your game

When the world fails to accept you, frowns over you,

Freedom in your mind brings you serenity,

A tide of content stability, in plenty.

When opinions and observations don't matter,

Following your heart is your only hammer.

Who are You? Who Am I?

Now breathing feels like a dip in ocean blues,

Rough waves will try to capture,

This is freedom, it will not break you;

Beautiful dolphins and orcas are here to rescue.

Independence is a choice,

Freedom is in the mind.

In truth, the one who is independent is not free,

And the one with freedom is likely to be independent.

Don't Compare

The ultimate goal of our existence is to be content in the end;

To live joyously, live the kind of life we dreamt.

As a child, we are asked about our ambitions,

Between education, work and responsibilities,

We often forget to care for ourselves;

Are lost and conscious even with best of friends,

Moments where we must enjoy,

We overthink and destroy.

Have you ever paused to notice,

Asked yourself the reason behind losing focus?

Are you starting to not like yourself?

Or feeling unloved, are you valued?

Is it troubling?

Are you comparing?

From the time we learn to speak,

Training for education, right behaviour in speed,

We are all compared.

Parents comparing us with siblings and children of our age,

Teachers nagging and doing the same;

Partners and spouses comparing lifestyle choices and finances,

The world compares colour, status, creed and religious masses.

To ace in studies,

Dancing, sports and activities,

Higher pay-checks, doctorate degrees to business earnings,

We are all compared.

This habit of comparing,

That people are very well wearing;

This bad habit that no one teaches,

It is inbuilt in us humans,

We think we are geniuses!

And so, the journey begins,

To compare self, wins.

No one will tell you it is a sin,

How much you love yourself, matters within.

We learn from observation,

From our school books, 'distinguish between's' and vocations,

Family and people around hyper like preparing for a do-or-die situation,

A daily routine,

Self-comparison has become a tradition.

When we start to compare ourselves,

We are letting others treat us the same,

Allowing them to compare us through their wicked lens,

As per their perspective, expecting us to change.

The world is busy,

Replicating a life better than their archnemesis,

Constantly chasing after, treating life like it is competition.

If you want to heal yourself and wish to be happy,

Accept yourself from within and truly;

Don't compare yourself with others,

When and if you do so,

You will hurt your wonders.

Remember, what you have, others don't,

What they hold, you may not need;

Prioritise yourself; it's the best deed,

Your wishes are in your hands, indeed.

When you compare yourself,

You give yourself authority to get oppressed,

When things don't go your way,

It makes you depressed.

Gather your inspirations,

Appreciate your present;

Indulge in self-improvement,

Achieve your aspirations;

'I am enough'

Capture these magic words in all your sensations.

Don't compare yourself,

For your confidence will shatter,

Self-esteem will defend itself by taking the shape of glamour.

Don't compare yourself,

For you will start complaining,

You will mentally degrade yourself, negativity seeping.

Don't compare yourself,

It is self-harming,

The way you treat yourself allows others to behave the same with you,

The world is always watching.

Don't compare yourself,

Look out for what you love; run after that,

Seek your authenticity, find it and wear it like a
green flag.

Everyone is unique, with their own purpose,

Discover yours; remember, no one is perfect.

Imagine a world where we create a loop,

We begin to accept people the way they are,
healthy or bruised;

Where we stop comparing people and
name-calling some as 'nobodys'

Children will see the real souls for who they are,
even in shade,

Compare less, and inspire the future to become a
happy place.

The Ultimate Dream School

Nestled in hues of bright, shiny and golden,

Skies wide, and hearts awoken.

A wonderland, with minds ready to board a flight,

A flight to where each day dawns with endless light.

Its entrance, like a mother's warm embrace,

Through hugs & goofy smiles, it assures security for the first-timers,

To parents, it offers hope, trust and wisdom's crest,

This magical institute is for all the eager, curious and blessed.

A sanctuary weaved in promises and care,

A place where dreams breathe in open air.

Here, even the halls echo of motivation and cheer,

Every corner, a memory, future bonds you will hold dear.

Walls adorned with stories, old, present and new,

Carving initials and dates with a protractor,

No polish, no chemicals can wipe away this memoir.

Of triumphs earned and passions pursued,

Classrooms bathed in young, energetic laughter,

A canvas of learning, where all are one and all looked after.

Desks hold not just books but dreams untold,

A treasure of knowledge, more precious than gold.

Teachers here are more than guides,

They show the path where the world resides.

With patience vast and hearts sincere,

They shape our futures, year by year.

Their words are not lectures but songs of leaders,

Kindling in us a boundless ladder of desires.

To think, to question, to dare and explore,

They identify talents, help recognise our interests,

And help us through limits to create a roar.

Of playgrounds that are joyful & freeing,

Where friendships blossom with time fleeting,

Art rooms whispering of colours and dreams,

Imaginations flowing like radiant streams.

Physical exercises and sports building motor skills,

Music classes teaching philosophies through hymns.

Discovering flags, stamps, nations and currencies,

For future world explorers, there is History and Geography.

Languages in abundance to learn and master,

It is the gateway for new horizons to conquer.

Science that connects you to the Earth and its creation,

Mathematics, so easy, everyone is a calculator!

Libraries stretching with words untold,

Unlocking the depths of imaginations and adventures,

Stories on humanity, emotions unfold.

Here all voices are heard,

Every thought and behaviour understood, answers treasured,

Turning each one that is unique into a wizard.

Differences here are celebrated, not shoved away,

Attributing skills of love, support and empathy,

Here, unity blooms each day.

Beyond academics, it coaches the heart,

Lift others high, to stand for the weak,

Learn the drift between need and greed.

The art of kindness and strength to face obstacles,

And not be afraid of the dark.

At this prestigious dream school,

Children care for the child within,

Trauma and hurt are healed,

Love and enlightenment now live, grow and function.

It teaches to value the humble, be gentle with every being,

To cherish every moment and find the goal you are seeking;

Till the mind, soul and heart are content,

To keep trying and give oneself more than one chance,

Respect above all is the greatest present.

This ultimate dream school is a happy place,

A place where failure is not the end,

Here, stepping stone is a lifelong friend.

Courage is sown and resilience is grown,

Every child's potential sits on a throne.

The ultimate dream school is out of the ordinary,

It is an emotion, a sacred space and a beautiful journey.

An institution that is contrary to force or control,

This school is a nurturing ground that makes us whole.

For this dream school lives in the heart and mind,

For everyone and anyone who wants to grow, play, jump and go wild.

It can be a child's forever happy place,

A legacy of love, fun and solace,

A wonderland, with minds ready to board a flight,

Where each day dawns with endless light.

Its entrance, like a mother's warm embrace,

This magical institute is for all the eager, curious and blessed,

The guidance of teachers here is the universe's grace.

Love

What is Love?

No, it's not, ‘baby, don’t hurt me’.

For it will hurt, sometimes only.

What is Love?

Definitely not a dove.

Valentine cards, expensive gifts and blushes;

It's not love if it is all a secret and hushes.

Not in romantic novels and top-rated movies,

Reality shows, music videos or classical beauties.

Learning the language they speak,

Cracking their likes, dislikes,

Keeping up with their favourite football teams;

Following and stalking wherever they go,

Do they believe in UFOs?

Listening to the music they love,

Struggling to enjoy the food they like,

What is their zodiac sign?

All these exertions for infatuations and crushes,

Dreaming of them, friends teasing, all mushes and blushes.

Is this really love?

Love is a feeling, a vibe,

You may not know swimming but are ready to dive.

A sense of security, safety, respect & happiness,

It is through profound interaction and conversations,

No trading of treatments and conditions.

More than you love yourself or your parents,

Above lust, satisfaction, no craziness;

It feels easy and simple,

Even if you rush in, Love is timelessness.

It is not about only surprising each other,

But putting in effort, because they matter.

When you allow yourself to be open,

Fun, happy, sad, lost or emotionally frozen;

When you are ready, yet exhausted and tired,

Let them see your darkest and kindest side.

If they accept you as you are,

It is you who they need and not just want,

They are the ones, rare like a star.

To not change you but grow together,

Letting in your flaws, care, anger, past and even fears,

No questions asked; they are all ears.

To support all the way, and just let you be,

If you feel the same, you are meant to be.

Grumpy in their absence,

Your entire world lights up in their presence.

When your heavy head hurts with worries and stress,

Their smile eases you out, like a bless;

After the worst day, or when really sad,

As soon as you see them, you instantly relax;

Every embrace, touch and kind word secures you,

This is Love, I can assure you.

When they admire you,

And not for the sake of it.

They read you well,

If you are angry, upset and even the mysteries you don't tell.

They cheer you on for your silliest requests and decisions,

Guide and lecture for your best, with good intentions.

They are your strength and never your weakness,

They may be an introvert or a sage for the world,

When with you they are foolish, dancing, funny, leaving you speechless.

Yes, I am in Love.

Nights filled with laughter,

Arguments and fights rarely occur,

Discuss, process, kisses and cuddles after.

Without them beside you, you cannot sleep,

At trips, occasions and events they can't make,

You miss them dearly and deep.

Overly expressive you become,

Sharing minute details; you are no more numb.

You are his princess,

He is your treasured companion for life, priceless.

You overindulge in doing things for him he likes,

Give all of yourself, not thinking twice,

He does the same for you without boasting,

It is not a compromise or a favour,

It is Love, full of hopes and adventures floating.

Only freedom, no insecurities,

Together you laugh reading your silly poems and
broken heart stories.

A warm embrace with no doubts and cracks,

Your trauma and triggers he understands and subtly grabs.

No keeping a tab on demands and supplies,

Being transparent, no filter, no lies;

You are no secret; the world is aware, you are his pride;

Long drives as dates, open sky and cheesy fries.

Of people you don't care,

Even silent dates you gladly share;

Phones you don't need to trace,

Trusting each other, as strong as waves,

He is my love, my happy place.

His slight sickness worries me,

For him, I can do things I would never do,

While the world feels I have changed,

Stating, 'You are not the same',

It is love, my dear,

And what a wonderful love I have gained.

Friendship

A bond both fragile and strong,
Not born of blood, yet closer than kin,
A treasure for the soul, a warmth within.
More than laughter and cheer,
Thriving in moments of storms that steer.

When life takes turn towards a frigid cold,
It's a hand to hold, a needed courage to go bold.
Respect is the soil where it grows,
A holy regard for the life it knows.

To honour their voice, opinions and beliefs,

To be present in their presence,

And hear them out when support they seek.

Loving them the way they are,

Appreciating the person they are, not who we wish them to be.

It's giving them space, yet standing near,

Trusting their choices and quelling their fear.

For no bond can flourish in judgement's shade,

In admiration's sun, it will never fade.

Secrets whispered under starlit skies,

Exchanging dreams softly, sharing words of advice,

Friendship is a story of laughter and tears,

Of triumphs celebrated and conquered fears.

Finding happiness in the simplest things,

Catching up at cafes, oh what joy it brings!

From unplanned adventures to quiet retreats,

Every second together is sweet.

Inside jokes that only you know,

Moments crafted, like rivers flow.

Your thoughts challenged, dreams encouraged,

Giving you checks of reality when your heart is caged.

Honesty wrapped in deep compassion,

Growing together in all aspects,

Through similar or variant perspectives,

Friendship is an eternal connection.

Trust is the heart of friendship, pure and deep,

A promise unbroken even when time is weak.

Secrets are safe in their charge,

Happiness and sorrows, equally shared at large.

Celebrating milestones, birthdays and success,

From graduations to weddings,

Shopping for matching clothes, sharing a dress.

With broken hearts, life feels unfair,

A friend is the healer that brings you out of your despair,

Through words that uplift and shoulders to lean on,

You are back on your feet when hope seems gone.

Love is the thread in friendship that weaves,

In the name of gifts, we exchange and receive.

Not bounded by terms, it asks for no fee,

It flows unbidden, organic and free.

Friendship rises when it faces rough waves,

Asks nothing more than happiness,

What a companionship it makes.

A quiet assurance, steadfast and true,

Like a mirror reflecting the best of you.

Care is the bridge that spans the divide,

A message, just once a week,

Is a gentle reminder of someone beside.

No act of kindness is small or vast,

The bond strengthens, until your last.

A 'hey', sent in the dead of night,

Sweet word of comfort, a guiding light.

Understanding, a foundation most rare,

The wisdom to listen and patience to bear,

Aware of their silence, the smile behind the pain,

Walking beside them through joys and strains.

For no friendship can thrive on monotony alone,

It's built on the wisdom that we have grown.

Through every quarrel and every sour moment,

It teaches us grace; it humbles our pride,

Thoughtfulness deepens, and you forever walk side by side.

Cherish your friends with all your heart,

With respect, love and empathy's embrace,

Friendship is a Happy Place,

A true timeless grace.

Bhaiya

My elder brother, my guardian, my guide,

Your steady presence is where I confide.

A looming shadow, both fierce and kind,

Like a tall, sheltering tree, Bhaiya, you are a harbour that's mine.

From the time I was born, you have been my light,

Bright star shining out even on the darkest night.

Each day filled with laughter and giggles,

Dancing on bed, listening to music, your footsteps I trail,

Through your quiet strength, I learned to prevail.

Admission at the institution, same as yours,

First day of primary school, oh what a day this was!

Prominent eyes, all on me as I entered the gate,

Recognising me and whose Sister I was,

Crazy fangirls that were your classmates,

Chased me down to hug and kiss,

Pulled my cheeks; which part did I miss?

Overwhelmed, confusion dawned on me,

An old teacher of yours approached slowly.

'Are you Gautam's sister'? She asked,

Nodding in agreement, I glanced.

A heartfelt story she shared that made me warm,

Of a little girl who couldn't breathe when she was born,

Scary and critical was her condition,

Worried, the girl's brother decided to take care of this situation.

Next day at his school's morning assembly,

He requested the entire school to pray for his baby sister's life,

The following day, she became all healthy and fine!

'That little girl is you, Tripti,

And the whole school wants to greet you'!

My cheeks even today get red,

Thinking of your unconditional love and words unsaid,

Happy, grateful tears run down my face;

Till this day, I thank God for making me your little sister,

Bhaiya, you are a parent in disguise; you are God's praise.

When I stumbled in youth, unsure and small,
You stood beside me, solid through it all.
At the age of seven,
When I was bullied by a boy at the playground,
Coming home and crying,
Explained how I felt threatened.

I decided to never go and play,
You took me by hand to the park next day,
The boy didn't come near me or around,
I ran, slid, swung and happily screamed aloud,
And forgot all about the boy and my sadness,
My excitement was total madness.

It is only now that I realised you had my back,
You handled the situation, met the boy for a chat,
Like the hero that you are in my life's story,
Many wars I have won because of your glory!

Like the time when I was a teenager,

Bhaiya, you were a patient teacher,

With wisdom to share,

Unspoken lessons laced with care.

You taught me to dream, to aim for the skies,

And wiped my tears, and my hope shined.

Oh, how I envied your strength, your might,

Yet you showed me the power of doing what's right.

Through your kindness and grace,

I passed through life's difficult maze.

A naive teenager that I was,

Bullied by boys like a pack of fox,

Troubled and tangled in my own thoughts,

You stood up for me; your action a fireball.

Respect I earned was the most precious gift from you,

And respect is what stays alive in my heart for you.

It is till this very date,

All the boys that have hurt me,

Are scared to come near,

Talk about your love, care and how you hold me dear,

They still admire you even in fear.

Your hands, rough from toil and play,

Taught me to build and outline my way.

In your quiet gaze, I saw the truth,

A silent protector through my youth.

Not all days were soft or sweet,

There were times we clashed; our tempers would meet.

But even in anger, I could always see,

An unyielding love tethered to me.

You taught me about music and the fun it brings,

Have even lied for me and taken me for a swing.
At ungodly hours you would take me for a drive,
Hanging out together with our friends, unbroken ties.

When there were decisions I couldn't take,
Your encouraging words and worldly experience,
Guided me to wake,
With exceptional knowledge and empathy,
You moulded me into the person I am today,
Look what you made!

As years unfurled and paths diverged,
Your wise words I can always hear.
In this mosaic of life, your role stands tall,
A cornerstone in the foundation of it all.

My happiest moments I have lived with you,
With the craziest of stories,
Laughing like monkeys,

Grabbing midnight munchies,

Spontaneous plans and long drives;

Attending concerts, hosting parties,

Lighting Diwali lamps, lights and dazzles,

Every second spent with you is special.

Bhaiya, you are more than a kin,

A spark where love and wisdom begin.

You always hold me together, without letting me know,

I have a depth of gratitude I never show.

What words can even suffice,

To honour our bond, precious and nice?

So, here's to you, my bhaiya, my friend,

A bond unbroken, a love without end.

For in this life, through all joys or strife,

You are, and will always be my happy place,

A forever, guiding light.

Self-Respect

Between priorities and obligations, it begins,

A whisper of worth in the heart,

Let your self-respect spin.

Like the roots of the banyan tree, deep in the ground,

Self-respect nurtures our spirit,

True strength is found.

Respecting oneself is to cherish the soul,

We recognise our value and feel truly whole.

In all relationships & associations, it sets the tone,

How we are treated and how we have grown.

More than honouring needs and voicing our demands,

It is about how we perceive and treat our own self that makes it grand,

This is how we build our legacy in the world that flourishes and stands.

We only settle for things in life that suit our worth,

For self-respect teaches us the true meaning of happiness and rebirth.

It is a trait we learn as early as a toddler,

Observing relatives and teachers,

Parents that nurture and foster.

Going after what and who makes us happy,

Sliding away from family, relatives, society that are rude and snappy;

Following our intuition and feelings,

Let self-respect take control and do the dealings.

Staying with the ones that love and secure us;

Where we feel we do not belong, where negativities lie,

It teaches us not to chase people or places we fear and makes us cry.

It is self-respect that teaches us to be ourselves always,

To get involved where we are not treated like slaves,

Believing, trusting and protecting ourselves through self-appreciation,

To never indulge in seeking outside validation.

Often seen as a dark factor,

Self-respect is not selfishness,

It is about shielding the self and looking after.

More than uplifting yourself when you are sad,

Less than thinking about yourself as superior to all,

When the world mocks you, insults that you lack,

It will remind you of the things you are great at,

Self-respect will bring you back on track.

In friendship, having self-respect is not wrong,

This circle of friends where everyone is free,

Valuation is equal, just like you and me.

If you are looked down upon by the ones you trust,

Snapped at, pressured, a cage-like feeling,

Hurt and sadness is what goes around in your gut;

To protect your heart and energy,

Self-respect makes sure these ties must be cut.

Friendships are built on love and esteem,

We lift each other up; together we dream,

We grow personally, and in careers we succeed,

It is a journey that must feel seamless, like a stream.

But friendships can falter when respect fades away,

When one feels superior or lost in dismay.

Starting over, we seek connections that nourish and grow,

Only kindness, love, support and laughter are all that we know.

In love's tender embrace, self-respect plays its part,

Healthy bonds begin at heart.

Boundaries set firm, yet gentle and kind,

Creating a space for fondness and attachment to bind.

When respect is mutual, love will feel bright,

Creating connections that shimmer with light.

To cooperate discreetly without losing our core,

The art of respect opens each door.

With a companion, we stand in our truth and grace,

Inviting deeper love into our sacred personal space.

Having foundations and values of friendship,

More intimate and sensitive is this companionship.

Remember you must, how you are treated within,

If happy you are with your inner dwell;

When the one you meet loves you and respects you,

More than you do to yourself,

Family and close ones are treated like gems,

And happiness is flowing; with each step, it excels,

In turn, this person will turn into your own Self-Respect.

Like a balm for the weary mind,

Self-respect raises resilience, leaving doubt far behind.

With each act of kindness towards ourselves, we find,

A sanctuary blooms within the heart and in mind.

Whether an entrepreneur, an employee or an employer you are,

Don't let comments and comparisons give you a scar.

Fight for yourself when you are wronged,

It is self-respect that will sharpen your sword.

Remember, that value and respect are not begged for but earned,

Start with yourself within,

This is an example set for the world to learn.

Nurture your worth with compassion and care,

Cultivate peace that's exceedingly rare.

In moments of struggle and doubt,

Self-respect scales memories of pride and skills you can count.

No longer a puppet in someone else's play,

Reclaim your voice; choose your own way.

Rise from the ashes of failure and pain,

Understand that growth often comes from strain.

In the mirror of the soul, where reflections reside,

Lies a treasure of worth that we often must guide.

Self-respect, a beacon, a flame burning bright,

Illuminates our path through the shadows of night.

Through feelings, dreams, wishes and fears,

Embrace this journey of self-respect through laughter and tears,

Self-respect is your mind's happy place,

Never let it disappear.

Self-Love

It is the depth of our being,

Here, inner beauty abides.

Self-love, that connects our soul to our heart and mind,

A journey within that makes us strong and kind.

Love yourself deeply, satisfy and honour your energy,

Recognise your value and follow your principles firmly.

It blooms like a flower in the warmth of the sun,

Nurtured by kindness, it flourishes – one.

In moments of doubt when the world feels unkind,

Self-love is the anchor that steadies the mind.

It teaches us grace in our flaws and our scars,

Reminding us gently, we are all shining stars.

Self-love is the guiding mirror that sheds all your mask,

It embraces your truth with each heartfelt task.

No longer confined by the judgements of others,

We celebrate our uniqueness; we are not runners.

It empowers us to stand tall and proud,

Helps us express who we are, no fear, no doubts.

It heals the old stories that linger and ache,

Transforming your pain into strength, it's a yummy cake!

Forgive yourself first, through compassion and patience,

If you don't love yourself, how will the world know of your essence?

The mistakes of your past are best where they lay,

Self-love makes you regret nothing,

For negative vibes, it's a pepper spray.

It creates your image with kindness for yourself to relish,

Reminds you of the happy days that you will forever cherish.

Self-love will give you a solid, confident stature,

No one's words or actions will hurt you, that's for sure.

In life's lows and highs, it will teach you to keep it together,

Love yourself to the length where you feel enough and looked after.

It keeps your surroundings, mind and body clean from dust,

Indulge yourself with time to feel and explore, you must.

Shopping, travelling, food, music, yoga, hobbies, research and studies,

If are therapeutic to your heart,

These are all self-love in a way and important for your growth and luck.

Love yourself through thick and thin,

And no self-doubts will seek in,

Comparing the self with anyone is self-abuse,

Understand that everyone is unique,

You are you, made for greater things,

When it's time, you will know your cue to spread your wild hues.

When we love ourselves, we teach others to see,

The beauty in empathy and compassion and how love should be.

It is a beautiful expedition; not just a phase,

A lifelong commitment, self-love is your own Happy Place.

Each step you take towards knowing who you are,

You illuminate a path of your desired future like a radiant star.

Celebrate this endlessly ongoing trip of profound personal evolution,

Embrace your flaws, plus points, ideologies and ethics like the ocean;

In the story of life where challenges pop up like a social media trend,

Self-love is the compass that will chaperon you till the end.

Knowledge

In this vast expanse of the human world,

Lies an endless galaxy of knowledge, both rare and heard.

It starts with a question, a spark in the dark,

A flicker of wonder ignites back in the yard,

From the buzzes of nature to the stars in the sky,

How deep is the ocean, what resides down below?

All about bodies, minds and souls that have windows,

Curiosity waves to reach out and fly.

Some are born gifted, with minds like a flame,

Absorbing the world each second, they are ever-evolving with many aims.

With an innate hunger for all that lives or what is true,

They hunt for answers and gain knowledge like a fresh brew.

Yet knowledge is not just a gift from above;

It's nurtured through effort, passion and a drive to know,

Through books, mentors, trials and errors,

Cultivating wisdom that grows through years,

Moving slowly to change the world, presenting a show.

Each lesson that is gathered, each truth is embraced,

Shaping understandings, enriching the space,

Knowledge is an abundant, happy place.

From history's echoes to science's might,

Knowledge empowers, makes us rich and defined.

With knowledge comes power to behold,

Breaking down barriers, it shapes and moulds.

It is responsible to lead paths that are bright,

Illuminates shadows with clarity,

If not done rightly,

It can break, brainwash and ruin the world's sight.

Knowledge is growth; a journey that opens eyes,

With insights through experiences, life and wisdom,

Travel, relationships, work, entertainment and fathom,

Everyone has a perception; no one is dumb.

Through discipline and practice, sharpen your tools,

Transform your drive into a powerful jewel.

Knowledge never fades,

It lasts and grows forever,

A precious treasure not one alone can capture,

To get to this world and be on top,

One life is not enough to hammer.

Yet with great knowledge comes responsibility too,

To share what we've learned and create a trusting crew,

For knowledge enriches our lives in full measure,

It is a boundless resource, a blesser.

Respect

When you love and don't want to hurt,

You hurt as a reaction, and within you cry out and sense the dirt.

Your intentions towards someone are pure,

It is more than getting liked; they are important to you,

You want to make them feel happy and secure.

Like relationships built on trust,

From a friend sharing secrets only for you to keep,

To a stranger pouring out his dreams, sadness and schemes when weak,

Be discreet and not let the word out and cheat.

Giving credit to the founders,

Upset is your mood, and still, you send out flowers,

Not arguing and fighting back in front of guests and crowds,

Space you need to give even to the proud fools that don't own their confounds.

Keeping quiet when there is a burst of anger,

To let out a quiet sigh when you are right but the other wants to banter,

Not remarking during singers that underperform bangers;

Halt sharing opinions on how to live a life when you are no master,

Commenting on someone's work when you are no professional,

Confidence you want to shatter?

Accepting each one as they are,

Being non-judgemental will take your love far;

To obey with a smile for the sake of your bond,

Listen to your own heart over advice from a frogpond.

Blood for blood; respect is not taught,

It is instilled in minds that are curious and broad.

It begins with the recognition of worth,

Worth of your words, nature and your presence in someone's life.

If you are looked up to and why,

Have you made a difference or impacted the wild tides?

It is not a birthright but a ritual that is earned,

Unless you are born to a king or are the universe's code,

Respect is given through the gratitude gesture of being bowed.

With a pinch of kindness, knowledge, grey-hair experience and a great networking history,

Topped with hard work, a success rate card and persuasive mystery,

Farther than materialistic thoughts and phoney actions,

Respect is something that will touch your heart in a fraction.

Acknowledging stories,

Of perceptions and their beautiful journeys,

From the laughter of children to the wisdom of age,

Respect is the ink that denotes a sage.

It flourishes through conversations spoken softly,

A bridge that connects us when we are lonely.

Respect is a listener that hears with observation,

Valuing each one without discrimination.

Regardless of where you come from,

What matters where you are today;

It is a golden thread that ties all relations,

Respect will make this world a happy place one day.

It is in every culture, tradition and languages unique,

Respect is one medium that unites the world; it's a real treat.

It thrives in happiness and success,

Makes you think about the ones that matter,

When appreciated while you think of yourself as less.

Respect is not always passive,

It stands up for what is right,

It can fool the ones who beg for it,

Blinding egos until hit with the truth's light.

In the face of oppression and voices unheard,

Respect fuels courage, empowering wizards.

Its importance is a teaching that is needed in schools,

With children becoming empathetic and not just cool,

Imagine what could the future look like,

A world that is free from thoughts, cruel.

From speaking out for others when silence prevails,

To uplifting the fallen when their hope seems to fail,

Respect is a grand commitment; it can break or upscale,

What a happy place this world would be to live in,

With people kind and vibrant,

Wearing respect as a brand,

Only love and appreciation shall it attract,

Respect is thus a remarkable impact.

Influence

Like a whisper, it stirs the stillest air,

Seedling thoughts that are beyond compare.

Silent, subtle and vast,

Influence is a force that shapes and futures it casts.

Can bend the rivers and stoke the flames,

If executed carefully,

Can carve on gold your name.

World that is so detailed and large,

Every thought in our brain is an influence
parched.

From appearance to behaviours,

Based on our parents and friends with experience;

Past habits to Future endeavours,

We change and grow as per what is a 'required'
convenience.

Dreams we had as children,

To adults with boards hanging our visions;

Acting and reacting as the world takes a tour,

Planning vacations based on a marketer's
experience brochure.

From our hair, head, eyes to toes,

It is influence that we are selling today as a
disguise,

Hiding the craving for appreciation, we always act
surprised.

What and how do you perceive it,

Influence becomes and takes a whip.

It can teach, craft and make you fly,

Do your due diligence, or you may cry.

Take a dip and indulge in your goal,

Choose the prize rightfully,

Influence can truly guide your soul.

Good influence shares with transparency,

Not commands and demands, as if hungry for money;

It can strengthen your will,

And foster care,

Keeps you grounded as well as aware.

Like water, it is seamless with depths that inspire,

A source for growth, for whatever you aspire.

Darkness too can charm the eye,

A voice as sweet as honey's lie.

It drapes in cloaks, fleeting with comfort and ease,

With false promises, it purely aims to tease.

Pulling you away from who you are,

Filling information that is far from the truth,

Making your relationships hard with scars.

With the wrong influence,

Loved ones and most trusted can be lost,

It will trap you under the strangles of life's cost.

A siren's call, a fading star,

Bad influence clings on,

Until you open up to reality,

And claim your spar.

The key lies not in haste or rush,

Only in the blessed art of hush.

Observe the roots from where it breeds,

And question where its current streams.

Does it align with your values that you hold dear,

Or strikes them with the bombs of doubt and fear?

Good influence calls out your best,

It is happiness you feel in your chest;

It won't demand your blind consent,

Or change what life has meant.

It seeks no gain from your ascent,

Rather will create a lovable, secure nest.

Guard your heart, and keep it free,

From influence that bends the knee.

For those too quick to dance to tunes,

May find themselves in chaos soon.

To not be swayed is strength refined,

A naive heart with an alert mind.

Remember the values and principles you were bestowed with when born,

Attach to them deep, like anchors breaking storms.

The world is vast with voices loud,

Lucidity is the rarest shroud.

Differentiate the truth and tread with care,

Ultimately, passing trends will leave you bare.

Empathy

Take a moment to pause,

See through another's eyes, glance.

Dare your heart to lean,

Feel the language that is tender and unseen;

Tears will shed from unspoken dreams.

The world is too quick to judge and divide,

Empathy will teach patience, to wait beside.

Step outside of our own skin,

Embrace the struggles that others live in.

From sorrows or sharing their glee,

Discover bonds that set hearts free.

Just listen, don't speak,

Be present; don't jump to prove,

Walk the rhythm the other one grooves.

Adventures will be shared,

Bringing joy and pain,

Cultivate the art of understanding,

You will learn to sustain.

When you connect through deeper roots,

Common ground you will find to appreciate each other,

Even in dispute.

It will make you think before you speak,

To forecast reactions from your mind's peak,

Thoughtfulness will be your strong pursuit,

Like a magician, you will fix moods.

Listening is a skill so rare,

Can vanish with age, and no one will care.

Through empathy, you will gain control,

Listening and observing would be at your core.

You will scare yourself and other trolls.

It teaches you to prioritise,

And when to be unbothered.

An aid in digging a box of causes,

With blurred expressions of history,

To maintain the legacy with stupid excuses,

Shaking emotions unspoken,

Observing their anger, reactions terribly chosen.

Entering their head,

For truth to declare;

Empathy will let you travel in their tale,

Make you wise enough to never leave a trail;

Only allow you to hold it tight with elegance,

Empathy is a profound secret to balance.

It is not be confused with sensitivity,

Empathy is vigilance, not slippery.
To empathise is a beneficial gain,
At personal, professional and societal scales;
Allowing one to shed their strains,
Everyone wins this unbiased game.

To be empathetic is to justly rise,
See the world through distinctive eyes.
It fosters bonds where walls once grew,
Turns strangers into friends with a simple view.

In its embrace, no one's alone,
Empathy strengthens the ties of the soul.
Lightening the burdens we quietly bear,
Revealing to the world that you care.
It teaches compassion,
An art to ace,
A path towards consideration,
Empathy is a happy place.

As it flows, one heart to another,
Creating a connection like no other;
In acts of concern and gestures small,
We weave a rich tapestry that honours us all.

This world is run by jealousy and strife,
Empathy is the thread that can stitch lives,
Reach out to those lost in despair,
And offer your heart with genuine care.
Take a moment to pause,
See through another's eyes, glance.
Dare your heart to lean,
Feel the language of empathy,
Tender and unseen;
And tears will be shed from fulfilled dreams.

Priorities

In the rush of the day,

We juggle our tasks in a frenzied ballet,

Hours go by, time slips away.

With a list that grows longer,

From tasks to wishes to decisions, we ponder,

Often, we feel exhausted and lost,

The art of prioritising can help lighten the cost.

First, seek your intention,

Collect all the 'why's' behind each goal,

What truly matters to you?

What feeds your soul?

In the quiet of the morning,

Take time to reflect,

On values and passions that you must protect.

For priorities shift like the sands on the shore,

What once held your focus may matter no more.

So, tune into your heart;

Let it guide your way,

Discern what is vital in the light of each day.

Pen down your thoughts;

Let them flow through every page,

Create a list specific and compact,

Wear a crown over your own sacred stage.

From urgent to important,

Categories you must form,

Through a structured approach,

Your mind will be calm.

Tackle the pressing with vigour and strength,

Seek the treasures that bring pure enjoyment.

For life is not measured by tasks left undone,

Moments of joy and relationships give reason.

Think of your precious time,

How do you want to spend it?

Keep boundaries in place,

Pretension will get you troubled and hazed

Allocate hours to what matters most dear,

Do not commit in haste and emotions,

Guard your words,

Hold your promises near.

In the dance of existence,

Learn to say no,

Cut off distractions and noises that hinder your flow.

Every 'yes' uttered takes a piece of your heart,

Choose wisely; let the purpose be impart.

Yet, life's currents can shift in a breath,

What seemed like a priority may lead to new depths.

Adaptability must be embraced;

Let go of the things that you grip,

Flexibility is like a balanced ship.

Revisit your list as seasons unfold,

What once felt essential may no longer hold gold.

In this journey of living,

Be gentle and kind,

Think of yourself and your choices;

Clarity will bind.

Reflect on the time passed at the end of each day,

What brought you fulfilment?

What led you astray?

Celebrate victories, all big and small,

Each step you take is your Salvador.

Acknowledge your stride,

Pray with gratitude and share your pride,

Prioritising wisely brings peace inside.

With purpose aligned and intentions set clear,

You will navigate life with courage and cheer.

The Grapevine

Eager lips unwind the stories,

Each line spiced with ease;

Weaving tangling webs, cruel and unkind,

Grapevine extends to connect more curious minds.

It unites the foolish who believe everything they hear,

Piles of lies break through; the truth begins to die.

What once was a whisper grows into a tradition,

A hoax reimagined, embellished and more.

In the heart of the circle where tattletales dwell,

An impatient hunger for drama; they thrive on the swell.

Gossip wears many faces and is often sweet,

Friendly exchange over a coffee meet.

It hides under the emotional sheets of concern,

Luring you to share secrets, a much-alleged yearn.

In our quest for connection, we overlook,

Scandals can ruin bonds that are grounded and good.

For every communication that travels too far,

Can leave us estranged from those once held dear.

Words hold a power that cuts like a knife,

They shape our perceptions and alter our lives.

A rumour can shatter a reputation so dear,

Leaving scars on the heart that linger for years.

For behind every rumour lies someone's pain,

Misaligned truth that brings heartache and strain.

Be wary of the shadows where gossip roams,

Each careless word can feel far from home.

Let's silence these traits that poison our minds,

When given a news, keep it to ourselves and unwind;

To think, if the information is vital to share,

Or can be ignored and let out of the hair.

In this world of grapevine, we stand at a crossroads,

Whether to join in the chatter to look cool,

To lighten our load,

Or to not indulge and keep walking away,

Not allow temptation to come our way.

Follow the golden silence that speaks only volumes,

Take the responsibility to choose from happiness or fumes;

Uplift or tear others down,

To spread seeds of empathy or wear a black crown,

To face the mirror with pride or live in shame,

Walking on the right path,

Is to honour our own values and shield our name.

Let us begin to be vigilant in what to convey,

Speak with warm intentions and brighten the day;

In honesty's light, we find strength to unite,

Transforming and letting out words that don't bite.

In this rumoured era with fairytales spun with ease,

It is time to foster a culture and cultivate trust;

And wear hearts on our sleeves.

For when we choose kindness over gossip and strife,

To honour life and voices of all,

Be a true friend, at beck and call.

Grapevine can't be erased forever,

It will live like an unintentional err;

Let's pick words that don't leave a trace,

Create a beautiful world without gossip, a Happy Place.

Time

Like a river that gleams beneath the sun's gaze,

Time winds onwards, even in space.

It carries our laughter, sorrows and dreams,

Creating moments of wonder and historic human routines.

Gives chances in abundance to try, succeed, fail and learn,

To grow, experiment, run and burn.

Time is a gift we don't realise we need,

It is the sorcerer of the universe,

Spells in speed.

Summer, Winter, Monsoon, Autumn and Spring,

Surprises attached to all seasons and climates,

Celebrations to the world it brings.

When life is filled with happiness and progress,

The time is praised and thanked for its greatness;

Blessings are showered even to the dead;

A mistake by and from human doings, it takes blame,

Cursing the timing of destiny,

From sages to astrologers, ironically, time predicts fame.

Time is a crafting experience,

Every second, moral message it ticks.

It is the beginning and the end,

Time is obligated to be spent.

One cannot save it for later,

Anxiety-driven commercials induce the thought of now or never;

Utilise it for personal gains, Time serves as a pleasure.

If not prioritised as per societal perceptions, you are wasting it,

Building in silence, indulging in leisure, you will be respected,

Time should be harnessed to fulfil dreams,

Do not take it for granted.

For the materialistic diggers, it is on the run,

Time is money;

If you are content with the present, it pauses,

Laying on the beach bed at dusk,

Time is fancy.

It stops in our mind,

Such as people in love, behaving blind;

If not valued, it will leave you behind.

From the innocence of youth to the wisdom of age,

Writing stories on a boundless page.

Every heartbeat preaches us to embrace,

The fleeting nature of time's tender grace.

Sitting idle in silence, holidaying with parents,

Exploring life with siblings, endless;

Hustling at work, diligent to make a name,

Long list of wishes to claim,

To cherish happiness and each tear,

Getting acquainted with new people,

Catching up with old friends for a beer,

In the stillness of twilight, when shadows grow long,

We ponder memories that shape our own song.

For time is a mirror reflecting our past,

Wedding albums of our parents, how beautiful they looked,

Time fled fast;

Nostalgia hitting emotional spots,

Emphasising that childhood birthday parties were a blast,

Time is a canvas where reminiscences are painted to last.

Through stories of ancestors who weathered the storm,

Finding strength in their voices; their wisdom warns;

Magical stories from mythology keep us warm,

A lot to learn and get inspired from the chapters of wars.

Seizing the present for the future,

Preserving seeds, minting biodiversity, saving nature,

Carving on walls to parching on paper,

Cameras with rolls, filming in danger;

Restoring books digitally for an aim greater,

Refurbishing momentous structures,

Researching the universe, giving names to its maker,

Keeping the foolish world busy through entertaining players;

Combats winning economy, destroying habitats,

Soldiers bruising.

We are chasing time to hold and capture.

For time teaches patience and nurtures the soul,

It has the power to heal and control.

Time is a phantom that shapes us into who we are,

Limitless opportunities it brings with conditions, bizarre.

Time is the Sun,

Every dawn brings chances anew,

To rewrite stories, to imagine, dare and pursue.

Grip it with joy; don't race,

Without Time, there would never exist a Happy Place.

A Happy Place

Each time, impacts deeply,

Calm and fulfilled with tranquillity,

Feels like solace,

In mind, heart and body.

Past is where it best lies,

Nothing here can hurt you.

Negativity is for the dump yard,

A happy place has no scars.

Pretty dreams travel,

Music is the gift that unravels.

Where the colour of your skin doesn't matter,

No dusty secrets one can scatter.

Self-protection at wide,

Siblings are for life,

In times low and tides high,

Respecting each other in pride.

See through others' eyes,

Hurt, hope and goodbyes.

Everything you love is here,

Nature, a gift so dear,

A pledge to protect it and hold it near,

Open your eyes; everything around you is sheer.

Where every creature, great or small,

Is cherished, valued, loved by all.

Cognisance finds peace here, at last,

Time just melts, doesn't go by fast.

A happy place is where the heart is,

Full of cheer and pure bliss.

Where the mind is calm and thoughts are blank,

Spaces are full for no doubts or traps.

The heart is content letting the smile but speak;

For the dreams we have and the wishes we seek,

A Happy Place is all we need.

9 789363 300842

Printed by Libri Plureos GmbH in Hamburg,
Germany